To Uncover Your Niche

To Uncover
Your Niche

Jack Blackhall

Bald and Bonkers Network Academy

CONTENTS

CONTENTS

First Printing, 2024

ISBN: 979-8-8691-3815-6
EISBN: 979-8-8691-3816-3

Introduction

In the dynamic landscape of contemporary business, the prevailing trend centers around entrepreneurs venturing into their own businesses. However, a common misconception among budding business owners is the belief that the mere establishment of a website is the golden ticket to success. While having a dedicated online presence is undeniably essential, it does not encompass the entirety of what is needed for a flourishing business. Regrettably, a significant number of new business proprietors underestimate the commitment of time and energy required to meticulously research a niche, a critical step in determining its viability and potential profitability.

At the core of building a resilient foundation for a prosperous online business lies the identification of a lucrative niche. Crafting tailored content, products, and services for this niche and strategically positioning oneself within the market are pivotal steps. Selecting a profitable niche is paramount for achieving the level of success and financial gains that render daily efforts meaningful.

Amidst the fervor and passion for online entrepreneurial pursuits, the crucial role of research often gets overlooked. Notably, successful global companies dedicate considerable time to market research before introducing new products. Unfortunately, a considerable number of new business owners bypass this crucial step, investing resources in product creation and launch without validating market interest.

The pathway to success in your online business begins with pinpointing a paying market.

Developing a product tailored to that market and executing a targeted marketing strategy yield optimal results. Effective niche marketing strategies are intricately linked to comprehensive research and the cultivation of robust relationships with potential customers in your chosen niche.

While there is an abundance of popular niches to choose from, not all guarantee profitability. While generating some income with budget-conscious customers is possible, the real financial rewards lie in catering to individuals willing to pay reasonable prices for genuine solutions to their problems. This approach lays the groundwork for a sustainable and successful online business.

Success in the online realm involves the cultivation of happy and loyal customers who consistently return. Thorough research ensures that your time and energy contribute to the establishment of a viable business. Without this foundational step, efforts invested in setting up a website, creating products, and selling them may prove futile. Choosing the right niche in a paying market is the key to earning the profits needed for success and achieving financial goals.

Understanding the Essence of a Niche

In the vast landscape of digital entrepreneurship, where the dream of running a thriving blog or website beckons, the initial choice of a niche emerges as a seminal decision in shaping the trajectory of your online venture. This foundational decision extends its influence far and wide, permeating through the very design of your site, defining the nature of your content, and dictating the kind of audience you attract. Even before you power up your computer, the choice of your niche lays the groundwork for potential monetization avenues. While there's no rigid concept of a wrong niche, the reality is that some niches prove more lucrative, while others present greater challenges. But what exactly is a niche?

Defining a Niche:

At its core, a niche can be described as a distinct area of interest or a group of products that cater to specific needs. For instance, an intriguing niche could revolve around the art of dog training, capturing the attention of pet enthusiasts seeking solutions to behavioral challenges. On the other hand, a product-focused niche might center on the fascinating realm of electric lighting, attracting individuals in search of both information and physical products. Both these niches share a common thread—they address problems faced by people, whether it's seeking guidance on dog training or finding the right lighting solutions.

The Power of Micro-Niches:

Delving deeper into the niche ecosystem, the concept of micro-niches emerges as a strategic advantage for online businesses. Rather than targeting broad subjects, a micro-niche narrows its focus to specific areas, such as Husky dog training or solar garden lighting. In these micro-niches, individuals are searching for precise solutions, allowing businesses to tailor their offerings more accurately. By showcasing products on a website that align with the specific needs of the target audience, the likelihood of making a sale is significantly enhanced. Another noteworthy advantage of opting for a micro-niche is the abundance of possibilities. Even in today's landscape, one can discover profitable micro-niches with relatively low competition, offering a unique opportunity to enter a market, address a problem, and provide an unparalleled solution.

Niche Markets: A Lucrative Territory:

Zooming in on niche markets, especially the dynamic realm of micro-niche markets, unfolds opportunities for online business owners. These niches provide a fertile ground for finding business opportunities with minimal competition. The key lies in discovering micro-niches characterized by both low competition and a substantial audience actively searching for solutions. While the quest to identify such niches may present challenges, the potential rewards in terms of profitability make the pursuit worthwhile. Whether through monetization via informational products, physical products, or pay-per-click advertising, the avenues are diverse for those who navigate the niche landscape strategically.

Niche Marketing: Unveiling the Strategy:

Niche marketing, as a strategy, involves the intentional promotion of products or services to a select group within a larger customer base. This approach stems from the recognition that there are often unmet needs within the broader market, needs that may be overlooked by companies targeting the more significant customer base. If a business can fill that gap and cater to these specific needs, it opens the door to a potential market eagerly awaiting solutions and willing to pay for them.

Consider the sprawling niche of Internet Marketing, which encompasses various sub-niches like search engine marketing, PPC marketing, article marketing, Google Ads, and more. These sub-niches can be further refined to include even more specific markets. For example, within the PPC marketing niche, businesses may focus exclusively on Google Ads or Yahoo Search Marketing. The growth of these particular niche markets is driven by an increasing demand for more information and resources tailored to specific business needs. This demand is often unmet by businesses targeting the larger Internet marketing market. Businesses specializing in article marketing may not cater to the needs of PPC marketers, and vice versa. Niche marketers recognize these nuances, enabling them to address the unique problems facing their target markets directly.

Navigating Niche Saturation:

Over time, niche marketing has evolved into a primary strategy, driven by the acknowledgment that the broader landscape of Internet marketing is becoming oversaturated with marketers and their products. This saturation poses challenges for businesses aiming to earn profits within the vast Internet marketing market. The entry barrier becomes even more formidable for newcomers, as established Internet marketers boast loyal customer bases that trust both them and their products. Consequently, targeting specific niches within the broader market becomes not just a strategy but a necessity for those seeking a competitive edge.

Diversification for Success:

Successful Internet marketers often embark on a journey of diversification, targeting different niches, some seemingly unrelated. The formula for success lies in diligent research to identify profitable niche markets, selecting appropriate domain names, building websites, and launching targeted marketing campaigns tailored to specific niche target markets. This proactive approach enables them to carve out profitable segments within various industries, ensuring resilience and adaptability in the ever-evolving online landscape.

Beyond Marketing: The Versatility of Niches:

While the term "niche" may initially evoke associations with marketing, it extends far beyond this realm, encompassing diverse areas such as dogs, gardening, home décor, writing, and more. The flexibility of niches becomes evident as any market can be systematically broken down into smaller, more manageable niches, either based on the nature of the product, the characteristics of the target audience, or a combination of both. The crux lies in identifying unsatisfied needs within existing markets and delivering valuable solutions that resonate with potential customers. In a landscape where new niches continually emerge, the possibilities are nearly limitless. Choosing the right niche for your business, amidst this abundance, becomes a process marked by strategic analysis and alignment with your unique offerings and expertise.

3

Unraveling the Profundity of Niche Exploration

In the labyrinth of entrepreneurial strategy, savvy business owners discern the potency of aligning their products and services with a specific niche of customers. This astute approach necessitates an intricate dance with market research, a meticulous choreography centered on unraveling the nuanced consumer behavior exhibited by the target audience within that chosen niche. The compass guiding these enterprises becomes a profound understanding of the needs, concerns, and desires intricately woven into the fabric of their niche.

As the research journey unfolds, revealing a genuine interest from consumers in the niche product or service under consideration, the orchestration of a diverse array of items for sale commences. This strategic symphony aims to cater to the diverse segments within the niche, employing various price points as the instruments that resonate with the symphony of consumer preferences. Acknowledging the multifaceted nature of niches is paramount, recognizing that certain products wield a broader appeal than others. For instance, within the realm of golf, products tailored for beginners might elicit a far-reaching interest compared to the niche seeking advanced golf information, where aspirations to become professional golfers drive the demand.

Strategic focus on products tailored for beginners emerges as a judicious move, fostering sales amplification based on volume. By offering a lower price point that resonates with a more extensive customer base, the likelihood of conversions is heightened. However, even within the niche of advanced golf enthusiasts, the exclusivity and high-level insights you can provide hold the potential to command a premium price. Crafting courses, coaching programs, multimedia packages, or exclusive membership programs for advanced students becomes not just a service but a premium experience, especially when positioned as an expert within the niche. The correlation between credentials and pricing underscores the reality that the more expertise you possess, the more you can command for the products and services offered within your niche, always tethered to the realm of reason.

Maintaining a price point within reason is a delicate balancing act, resonating with the pulse of the niche market. Navigating the landscape of finding the right niche transcends a quest for mere profitability; it's a nuanced exploration into understanding what motivates consumers to make purchases and how much they are willing to invest in resolving their problems. A profound understanding of the average price consumers are willing to pay becomes the lodestar guiding market entry decisions. If the prevalent average stands at $29.95, introducing a $39 product demands a compelling rationale for the premium.

Your credentials, expertise, and the added value offerings become the narrative that helps dissolve customer doubts, convincing them of the worthiness of the extra cost. This persuasive dance, however, requires a comprehensive understanding of the competing offers available in the market. Diligent research within your niche unveils not only its viability but also the willingness of users to pay premium prices for exclusive insider information.

A pivotal consideration during niche research extends beyond mere pricing dynamics to the customer life cycle within the niche. While customers may commence their journey as beginners, the evolving trajectory often propels them towards seeking intermediate or advanced information as they progress. Understanding this life cycle becomes the gateway to sustained engagement and a continuous cycle of sales. The age-old principle of niche marketing, the 80/20 rule, holds its ground, signifying that a substantial proportion of profits emanates from a smaller segment of loyal customers.

Exemplary customer care becomes the cornerstone for fostering regular purchases and an open receptivity to new products and services that seamlessly align with their evolving needs. Automation emerges as a silent ally in the realm of niche marketing, paving the way for a seamlessly orchestrated process with preloaded offers housed within an email marketing platform. This automated symphony delivers a harmonious stream of offerings to customers and prospects, ushering in a paradigm of around-the-clock income generation.

Honing in on a single niche market and orchestrating focused efforts becomes a transformative journey, turning visitors into not just customers but loyal patrons on your email marketing list. Niche markets, akin to a masterpiece, offer the unique advantage of possessing a distinctive product that can seamlessly continue to orchestrate sales for extended periods—weeks, months, or even years. Once the overture of a successful product resonates, the symphony endures, with the conductor's role involving a continuous effort to direct traffic to your sales page.

It's imperative to recognize that every niche is a unique composition, characterized by distinct needs, nuanced price points, and intricate consumer behaviors. Thorough research before choosing a niche emerges not just as a prerequisite but a symphony conductor's prelude, setting the stage for an opulent performance. This informed approach not only aids in setting realistic goals and expectations but ensures that your time, energy, and resources are not merely spent but elegantly invested as you embark on the grandiloquent journey of launching your business into the dynamic and ever-evolving landscape of niche marketing.

4

Decoding the Alchemy of Profitable Niches: A Comprehensive Exploration

Embarking on the journey of creating a product or service is a strategic endeavor that demands a prelude of thorough market evaluation. Before delving into the construction of a website or the production of content, an essential precursor lies in discerning the presence of an audience willing to embrace what you offer. This pivotal moment necessitates contemplation on the monetization strategy, intertwined with the question of whether the chosen niche aligns seamlessly with the envisaged business model. The stark reality is that not all niches are created equal in terms of profitability.

Unraveling the Profitability Enigma

The tapestry of niche profitability becomes discernible when one delves into the realm of monetization options. Among these, advertising surfaces as a viable avenue, involving the placement of banner ads or Google Ads on your website. However, this avenue, while common, often proves to be the least lucrative. Every click on an ad leads visitors away from your site, raising questions about the sustainability of this approach. Moreover, the viability of this strategy hinges on advertisers' willingness to pay for your traffic, demanding an intricate dance where they must derive more significant benefits from your visitors than you do.

Adhering to a nuanced understanding of advertiser dynamics unveils that profitability often hinges on the nature of what they sell. Advertisers who sell products retain the lion's share of profits from each visitor, establishing a paradigm that aspiring niche owners aim to replicate. The avenue to achieve this lies in crafting one's product, ideally a digital offering such as an eBook, or engaging in affiliate marketing by promoting products created by others. Alternatively, services can serve as a viable monetization route.

A critical consideration before choosing a niche revolves around the speed at which products within that niche can be sold, as this significantly impacts advertising fees. Niches with a plethora of sellable products often emerge as the most lucrative, attracting advertisers willing to pay a premium to appear on your website. The profitability of a niche, therefore, becomes intricately linked to the diversity of products available for sale within it.

For instance, selecting a niche like "Fortnite" may prove less lucrative due to limitations imposed by its nature as an online video game owned by Epic Games. The constraints include the inability to sell proprietary merchandise, leaving only options like 'guidebooks' that may not command substantial financial returns. Advertisers, recognizing the limitations, might hesitate to place relevant ads on such websites, leading to diminished click rates and revenue potential. This underscores the importance of assessing the product landscape within a niche before deeming it profitable.

Unraveling Profitable Niches

Certain niches inherently promise profitability by offering an investment avenue for customers. For instance, a blog centered on investing holds allure, as people are willing to pay to acquire knowledge that has the potential to yield financial returns surpassing their investment. Similarly, niches related to business, where individuals invest in online courses to learn money-making strategies, align with this profitability principle.

Another breed of profitable niches comprises those promising to bring about measurable life changes for customers. The value proposition here hinges on enhancing people's lives in tangible ways, compelling them to invest in products or services that pledge transformative outcomes. The fitness niche serves as a prime example, where individuals willingly spend on books or equipment with the belief that it will lead to improved health, confidence, and overall well-being.

Considering the price points of products or services within a niche is paramount. Niches featuring higher ticket items inherently carry the potential for more substantial earnings. For instance, a niche focused on sports cars has the capacity to yield significant returns. Similarly, travel blogs catering to travel agents and online travel platforms can command higher advertising fees. In the absence of an overtly profitable niche, creativity becomes the guiding force. This could involve auxiliary avenues such as helping people find hotels and earning commissions or building the site to later diversify into new areas.

The crux of niche selection lies in a meticulous evaluation of profitability indicators, including the value proposition, promise of investment, and the presence of high-ticket items. Even niches lacking these overtly lucrative characteristics can be navigated with ingenuity. Whether it's affiliate marketing, commission-based collaborations, or strategic expansion plans, choosing a niche requires a comprehensive understanding of its potential for profitability. Before taking the initial steps, it's imperative to ensure that all facets have been carefully considered, laying the foundation for a niche that not only aligns with your passions but also promises sustainable financial returns.

Expanding the Horizons of Profitable Niches

Delving deeper into the intricate web of profitable niches, it becomes evident that the landscape extends beyond conventional paradigms. The alchemy of niche profitability involves an exploration of diverse avenues that may not conform to traditional expectations. In dissecting the dynamics, it becomes imperative to consider the evolving needs and preferences of the target audience, unlocking new dimensions of monetization potential.

Beyond the realm of advertising and product creation, the realm of membership programs emerges as a potent force in niche profitability. Creating exclusive memberships, complete with premium content, specialized services, and a community of like-minded individuals, becomes a magnet for recurring revenue. By tapping into the desire for exclusive experiences, niche owners can establish a sustainable income stream while fostering a sense of belonging among their audience.

Affiliate marketing, often regarded as a cornerstone of niche profitability, can be elevated to new heights through strategic collaborations and partnerships. Building alliances with complementary businesses within the niche not only expands the range of offerings but also opens avenues for joint ventures, co-branded products, and shared promotional efforts. This collaborative approach not only enhances the value proposition for the audience but also amplifies the revenue potential for niche owners.

Diversifying the Monetization Tapestry

As the landscape of niche profitability evolves, diversification emerges as a key strategy to fortify revenue streams. While traditional avenues such as advertising and product sales remain foundational, the inclusion of complementary streams ensures resilience and long-term sustainability. Exploring avenues such as sponsored content, webinars, and online courses adds layers of depth to the monetization tapestry, providing diverse touchpoints for audience engagement and financial returns.

The integration of e-commerce within niche ecosystems unlocks new dimensions of profitability. Establishing an online store featuring curated products relevant to the niche not only generates additional revenue but also enhances the overall user experience. By seamlessly blending commerce with content, niche owners create synergies that resonate with their audience, fostering a holistic environment where users can explore, learn, and make informed purchases.

The Paradigm of Sustainable Profitability

In the pursuit of niche profitability, sustainability emerges as a paramount consideration. Nurturing a niche ecosystem that stands the test of time involves a delicate balance between monetization strategies, content relevance, and audience engagement. The quest for sustainable profitability necessitates an ongoing commitment to adaptability, staying attuned to evolving market trends, and leveraging emerging technologies to enhance the overall niche experience.

The cultivation of a thriving community within the niche becomes a cornerstone of sustainable profitability. Beyond mere transactions, fostering meaningful connections and interactions transforms a niche into a vibrant ecosystem where users not only consume content but actively contribute to its evolution. Community-driven monetization avenues, such as exclusive forums, premium memberships, and collaborative initiatives, solidify the bond between niche owners and their audience, creating a symbiotic relationship that endures.

Navigating the ever-changing landscape of digital entrepreneurship requires a dynamic approach to niche profitability. As technology evolves and consumer behaviors shift, niche owners must remain agile, embracing innovation and seizing emerging opportunities. The journey towards sustainable profitability transcends the confines of a singular strategy, weaving together a tapestry of diversified income streams, community cultivation, and a forward-thinking mindset.

In Conclusion: Crafting Your Niche Odyssey

This chapter unraveled the multifaceted dimensions of profitable niches, transcending the conventional boundaries of monetization. From the foundational elements of advertising and product creation to the nuanced realms of membership programs, affiliate marketing, and e-commerce integration, the exploration delved into diverse strategies for financial success within a chosen niche.

As you embark on your niche odyssey, consider this chapter as a compass guiding you through the intricacies of profitability. Tailor your approach to align with the unique attributes of your niche, infuse creativity into your monetization strategies, and remain attuned to the evolving needs of your audience. In the realm of niche entrepreneurship, sustainable profitability is not just a destination but an ongoing journey of adaptation, innovation, and community cultivation.

With these insights as your companion, venture forth into the expansive landscape of niches, armed with the knowledge to not only choose a profitable niche but to cultivate an ecosystem that thrives over time. Your niche is not merely a business endeavor; it's a dynamic tapestry waiting to be woven into a narrative of financial success, meaningful connections, and lasting impact. Let this chapter be your guide as you navigate the intricate pathways of niche entrepreneurship and embark on a journey where profitability meets passion.

5

Navigating the Niche Selection Maze: Crafting Your Path to Success

Embarking on your online niche business journey necessitates a thoughtful selection of the niche you intend to explore. To commence this process, take the initial step of jotting down your ideas for a niche, accompanied by a reflection on the underlying reasons driving your interest in it. The motivations behind choosing a particular niche can vary widely. While some are drawn to hot and trending markets, the allure of new and emerging landscapes comes with a caveat — the need for nimbleness and diligent effort to stay ahead of rapidly evolving trends.

It's crucial to recognize that trends, such as those spurred by prestigious events like presidential elections or the Olympics, can generate temporary buzz and demand for related memorabilia. However, the fleeting nature of such trends implies that engagement and profitability might dwindle once the event concludes. Niche markets centered around transient trends may necessitate a constant search for new, profitable niches.

Choosing the Timeless Path: Evergreen Niches

In contrast, niches that stand the test of time are known as evergreen niches. While these may not generate the same level of excitement as the latest gadgets or events, evergreen niches exhibit sustainability, offering the potential to keep your business thriving for years. The essence of an evergreen niche lies in the longevity of the products and services it encompasses, ensuring a consistent stream of profits over an extended period.

In addition to sustainability, the selection of an evergreen niche should align with your personal enjoyment and interest. Opting for a niche that not only endures but also captivates your interest ensures a fulfilling and enjoyable entrepreneurial journey.

Choosing Based on Personal Interests and Expertise

Many entrepreneurs find the niche selection process straightforward, grounded in their personal interests and areas of expertise. Being an expert in a chosen niche positions you advantageously, as your knowledge aligns with the needs and preferences of potential customers. If you personally invest in products within the niche, the likelihood of a paying market for those products increases.

However, a word of caution is in order. While personal interest and enthusiasm are crucial, assumptions about consumer behavior can be misleading. A well-thought-out idea might not resonate with the market without thorough niche research. New niche marketers often fall into the trap of creating products, websites, and more for niches with little to no value, either due to the absence of a paying market or misalignment with the target audience. Conducting comprehensive research, understanding the challenges and needs of potential clients, and offering viable solutions are pivotal steps in niche selection.

Selling as an Affiliate: A Strategic Entry Point

The easiest way to make money when you first start your business is marketing as an affiliate. Becoming an affiliate of top companies like Amazon provides you with access to millions of products that you already know are in demand. Depending on the reward system you choose and the products that you are selling in specific niches, you can start earning commissions as high as 15 percent. Many of the top companies, like Amazon and eBay, have their own affiliate programs that are administered in-house. Other companies run their affiliate programs through a marketplace that operates the program for them.

While the most lucrative way to make a profit in your niche is to create your own products and services to sell, there are several reasons why you might want to think about starting out with affiliate marketing. First and foremost, affiliate marketing is a way that you can become profitable soon after you start an online business. Plus, it takes less time and energy to get started. The products that you can sell through an affiliate program are a good indicator that the niche is a paying one. Affiliate marketplaces can also be a valuable place to conduct your research. They allow you to see precisely what people are buying, as well as how much they are willing to pay for the products and services. This can give you a good idea of how your own products and services will fit into the paying marketplace.

Starting out as an affiliate marketer can help

you avoid some of the common mistakes made in niche marketing, like setting a price point that is too high or too low or creating products that no one wants. Doing research will also help you identify gaps in your product and service offerings so that when you are ready to develop your own products or services, your final decision will be based on the research that you conducted as an affiliate marketer.

Another great reason to start off as an affiliate marketer is that you can learn a great deal about marketing, which can come in handy when you start to sell your own products and services. The affiliate marketing programs are usually run by a manager who is an expert in coming up with exciting offers, ideas, and graphics for their offers. Often, they will provide affiliate marketers with useful tips and hints that can help them later down the road when they are selling their own products.

Finally, the more streams of income that you can get for your business, the more profit you can make. Your commission checks may not be much to start with each month, but increasing your income will be up to you and how many products you can promote. Establishing multiple revenue streams contributes to the long-term financial health of your business, creating a robust and sustainable income model.

In conclusion, this chapter highlights the multifaceted process of choosing your niche. Whether navigating trends, opting for evergreen niches, or aligning with personal interests, each approach has its unique considerations. Additionally, entering the niche landscape through affiliate marketing offers strategic advantages, providing valuable insights and a streamlined entry into the world of online business. As you embark on this journey, remember that a well-researched and carefully chosen niche is the foundation of a successful online venture.

6

Embarking on Your Niche Adventure: The Art of Niche Research

Delving into the realm of your chosen niche requires a fundamental understanding of your target market, and the gateway to this knowledge lies in identifying the keywords employed by your audience. The first step is to discern the words they input into search engines, utilizing these keywords to explore topics and products related to your niche. This exploration not only unveils the pain points of your niche customers but also sheds light on the challenges they seek solutions for.

Unlocking the Power of Keywords Understanding the keywords associated with your niche is crucial for attracting a highly targeted audience actively seeking products and services aligned with your niche. Leveraging tools such as Google Ads Keyword Tool, a free resource, facilitates the discovery of specific words and phrases related to your niche market.

Google's Keyword Planner is another invaluable tool, offering insights into relevant keywords used by your target customers. Utilizing the data gathered from this tool, you can conduct comprehensive research into specific products, services, and solutions within your niche, refining your focus based on your area of expertise.

Identifying Profitable Keywords After pinpointing keywords associated with your chosen niche, the next step involves identifying those with the highest profit potential. The profitability of keywords can be assessed through three key metrics:

- Low competition
- High search volume
- Minimal cost/effort to rank high

Discovering High-Value Keywords Google Ads Keyword Planner empowers you to estimate potential visitor traffic for each keyword in your niche, revealing valuable insights into user preferences and related keywords. When selecting a viable and profitable niche, your research should be meticulous and targeted, ensuring comprehensive coverage of keywords and phrases potential customers might use to search for your products or services.

Analyzing Monthly Search Volume An essential aspect of keyword assessment is evaluating whether there is a substantial monthly volume of potential customers actively searching for the product or service you aim to sell. Additionally, determining if other businesses are already profiting from similar products or services can be accomplished using tools like Google's Keyword Planning Tool, Google, and Bing.

Organizing Keywords Effectively Organizing your keywords into groups is a critical step, involving the categorization of specific keywords and phrases. For instance, the keyword phrase "digital camera" can be further segmented into groups like "underwater digital camera," "underwater digital cameras," and "digital underwater camera." Each group should comprise keywords with a search volume of no less than 2,000 searches per month, aiming to understand prevailing mindsets within specific product or service categories.

Exploring High-Volume Keywords To delve deeper, select the top ten keywords from your research and strive to accumulate a total of 100,000 or more searches per month. Input these keywords into the Google Keyword Planner Tool to unveil more specific long-tail keywords, providing nuanced insights into user preferences.

Spotting Money-Making Keywords Identifying money-making words is the next crucial step. These buyer keywords, such as brand names, model numbers, color, cheap, buy, for sale, supplier, seller, etc., indicate a user's readiness to make a purchase. The more specific the search, the higher the likelihood that customers are prepared to buy.

Live Testing Your Keywords Live testing is paramount to gauging the potential profit of your keywords. Integrate keyword-specific content into your existing blog, website, or social media pages and assess their performance on search engines. Monitoring traffic and ranking positions will provide valuable insights into keyword effectiveness.

Competitor Analysis: Understanding the Landscape Conducting a thorough analysis of your competition is an indispensable step in niche selection. While most businesses have competitors, distinguishing between direct and indirect competition is crucial. Vigilance is essential when scrutinizing competitors, acknowledging their presence without succumbing to intimidation.

Quantifying Competitors in Your Niche To quantify your competition, perform a Google Search to determine the number of competitors targeting the same keywords. Analyze websites employing the same keywords in their URL, title, and anchor text. Tools like SEOmoz can reveal the number of backlinks your competition has, offering insights into their online presence.

Researching Competitors for Page Rank The difficulty of outranking your competitors depends largely on the Page Rank (PR) of their websites and relevant web pages. Assess the average PR of the top ten sites, aiming for a timeframe of under three months to rank for a keyword if the average PR is below PR3. SEO Quake is a useful tool for determining the average PR of the top ten websites for each keyword.

Evaluating Competition Creating a spreadsheet to evaluate competitors' PR is beneficial. Label one sheet "Preliminary" and another "Market Competition." List the top ten keywords in the preliminary sheet and create columns like "Site1PR," "Site2PR," up to "Site10PR" in the Market Competition sheet. Calculate the average PR, considering the highest and lowest PRs, to gauge competition difficulty.

Strategic Evaluation and Competition Analysis When confident in your niche choice, create reports, eBooks, articles, or white papers, offering essential information about the benefits of your business's products or services. Free content can serve as bait to engage potential customers, building trust and positioning yourself as an expert.

Considering Your Competition's Pricing Strategy If serious competition is apparent, subscribe to competitors' email lists to assess their pricing strategy. Observe whether they offer higher-priced products and services or consistently discount their offerings. Sustainable markets feature reasonable profit margins, allowing smaller players to enter and coexist with established brands.

Analyzing Search Engine Competition While

lower competition is generally favorable for search engine ranking, a niche devoid of competition may signal a lack of profitability. Balancing competition levels is crucial for niche selection.

Nurturing Meaningful Connections: Cultivating Enduring Relationships with Your Ideal Customer

Nurturing Meaningful Connections: Cultivating Enduring Relationships with Your Ideal Customer

Your ideal customer is not just a buyer; they are someone actively seeking solutions to their specific challenges, someone willing to invest in resolving their distinctive problems. The process of identifying and establishing connections with these ideal customers requires a nuanced approach, involving the delivery of valuable advice and solutions in the spaces where they naturally gather.

Fostering Connections through Free Content Offerings

One effective strategy in building connections with your ideal customer involves the creation of compelling free content that positions you as an authority in your niche. As potential customers recognize your expertise, they become more inclined to explore and invest in your paid content. It is imperative to perceive free content not merely as a promotional tool but as a sampler, enticing customers to delve into the complete package and laying the foundation for enduring relationships.

Strategic Development of Email Marketing Lists

Building an email marketing list emerges as a strategic maneuver to assess the viability of your chosen niche. Offering free newsletters or downloadable resources allows you to regularly market your products and services directly to your audience. The cultivation of customers' trust, grounded in your expertise, becomes the catalyst for them to consider and purchase the products you recommend. This iterative process establishes a framework for valuable, repeat interactions, fostering a sustained connection.

In-Depth Exploration and Surveying of Your Target Market

Following the selection of a profitable niche, an in-depth exploration into your target audience's pain points becomes essential. Understanding the critical challenges they face provides you with the insights needed to offer optimal solutions, elevating the profitability of your niche. This process involves not just addressing surface-level issues but delving into the underlying problems your audience encounters within the niche.

Leveraging Online Surveys for Insights

Utilizing platforms like Survey Monkey, Survey-Gizmo, and Google Ads enables you to conduct online surveys directly targeting your audience. Offering incentives, such as discounts or free downloadable products, enhances survey participation and enriches your understanding of the market. The goal is to amass over 1,000 responses, providing a comprehensive view that aids in shaping informed strategies for your niche business.

Acquiring Holistic Market Intelligence

Distinguishing itself from keyword intelligence, market intelligence gleaned from surveys offers a qualitative understanding that is accurate and confidence-inspiring for marketing and strategic decisions. The time invested in researching your niche and understanding your ideal customer pays dividends, not just in terms of identifying profitable products but also in establishing a foundation of trust and understanding with your audience.

Crafting an Informed Strategy for Niche Success

The process of building lasting relationships involves crafting a well-informed strategy, drawing insights from keyword analysis, competitor evaluation, and direct interactions with your audience. By understanding the intricacies of your niche, recognizing the pain points of your ideal customers, and actively engaging with them through various channels, you lay the groundwork for a successful, sustainable niche business.

Cultivating Meaningful Connections: Establishing Lasting Relationships in Your Chosen Niche

Now that you've strategically chosen a profitable niche, the journey towards success continues with the intentional cultivation of meaningful connections within that niche. Building lasting relationships involves actively engaging with key platforms like main sites, blogs, discussion boards, and forums associated with your niche. Take a deep dive into these resources, meticulously examining the prevalent topics being discussed, and extract the five most recurring issues that directly align with your chosen niche.

These identified issues serve as the cornerstone for generating valuable content, which can be seamlessly integrated into your newsletter, blog, and even a specialized free report. This content becomes not only a source of information but also a valuable incentive for potential customers to willingly share their email addresses, thereby establishing a direct channel of communication.

Consistency is key, and regular posting of relevant content across your social media networks becomes a fundamental strategy. Keeping your followers updated on your business activities not only maintains their interest but also encourages them to actively share and retweet your information, significantly expanding your reach within the niche community.

While the motivation for starting an online business often revolves around financial objectives, it's imperative to transcend mere monetary goals. The online landscape lacks the necessity for politeness, but genuine communication becomes the linchpin in retaining an audience. Initiating an e-course or enticing newsletter subscriptions provides a tangible opportunity to communicate regularly, laying the foundation for a relationship beyond a transactional nature.

Studies suggest that brand recognition and understanding require at least 17 exposures to a brand. Hence, creating a positive first impression becomes paramount, considering the scarcity of second chances in the online realm. Leveraging various channels, including email marketing campaigns, emerges as a lifeline for maintaining consistent communication with those interested in your niche.

Email marketing campaigns serve as invaluable resources, offering newsletters, special reports, and customized content to provide continuous value.

Segmenting your audience into specific lists, such as new customers, facilitates targeted communication strategies, ensuring the delivery of content relevant to each group's needs.

Retaining subscribers can be challenging, making it essential to offer consistent and valuable content. An e-course delivered through an autoresponder proves to be a structured and effective method for keeping communication lines open and building lasting relationships.

Beyond email marketing, social media networks play a significant role in relationship-building within your niche. Followers on platforms like Facebook can actively engage with your content, contributing to its reach within their networks. Harnessing this power can result in free traffic and increased sales.

Newsletters, as dynamic tools, enable you to provide your customers with regular and relevant content related to your niche. Covering common issues, FAQs, quizzes, and new product or service announcements, newsletters establish you as an expert without resorting to aggressive sales tactics. This approach not only builds relationships but also positions your brand favorably within the niche.

In conclusion, the success of your online business is intricately linked to the strategic choice of a profitable niche. Recognizing unmet demands in the market and addressing them provides your small business with a unique advantage. Offering unique or exceptional products allows you to reduce competition and carve a distinct space for yourself.

However, finding the right niche requires thorough research, patience, and the right tools. It's essential to ask the right questions and carefully understand the answers received during this process. The investment of time and effort in researching potential niche markets is fundamental to the success of your online business. As your business grows and profits increase, the rewards become evident, making the journey worthwhile.

www.ingramcontent.com/pod-product-compliance
Lightning Source LLC
Chambersburg PA
CBHW061719130726
47996CB00006B/2400